I0504508

# THE MONEY QUESTION ???

## Questions you are not asking.

## BENNETH FELIX.

# THE MONEY QUESTION
# ???

## Questions You Are Not Asking.

BENNETH FELIX                    THE MONEY QUESTION.
                                           ???

Published by Rebound Institute 2018

# LIFE IS A JOKE

What do you do when you think you have it all figured out but you have to deal with changes that knocks you off your feet?

What do you do when you thought you know how life works, what belongs to what, who to expect what from, yet you find that often the least amongst us holds the key to certain major questions you've been asking?

My dear, life is a joke. Don't take things too seriously. Don't get rigid in

your thinking. And don't restrict or constrict your experiences.

I am still in my own process of wealth accumulation. But I promise you you'll be thrilled by the insights you find within these pages. Yea, that's what I mean!

I didn't write the book because I've already attained, but for the sheer passion of being a voice to those who might not yet be privy to the ideas I expressed here, that I've experimented with myself and still put to work and which impact is registering.

After all, in the thoughts of Chimamamda N. Adichie, there is not a single story to any people, to anything and definitely to money.

The system of wealth creation is vast, you should know this. Even though it may have some basic underlying principles... howbeit, it's dangerous to tie it around some single story and dismiss any and everything that does not conform to that story.

So I employ you to explore this side of the story with me and see what you find.

# CONTENTS:

## Life is a Joke

# CHAPTER 1

# The money question!

## Money? Money? Money...?

"If you are serious about increasing your income, manage your time.

Set aside moneymaking time to focus your

mind and creative energy every day.

Become clear about what you want and be willing to tryout

new methods to earn money doing something you enjoy.

Create something that's you"

Les brown.

## The key to everything

Everything in life works by certain laws and order. And I am going to address most of these laws in detail at a later chapter. Certain principles work to bring about the manifestation of things, even though this set of principles are scarcely apparent in their functions, they however are the reason things work in that respect. Often you don't need to actually see or understand all about the principle in operation to accept and obey it, you just do!

You don't necessarily understand how the law of sowing and reaping operates, or how the seed germinates in the earth. You just obey it. You just sow your seed and let the law come into operation.

The wisdom therefore of *precision and focus* in realizing ones goals can never be overemphasized, cause by applying them in any subject matter you set yourself aside to excel in that quest. It is a functional law of its own. So is the law of Cause and Effect, as you shall see throughout this book.

The subject of moneymaking however is no different. We know how much our world associates hard work, grit and smartness as the single most reliable avenues for wealth creation. But this does not always go in the favor of everyone. This has not only been a course of concern over the years, it has also raised questions as to why that is.

So, in this work we shall be examining some questions that challenges status quo and examines personal prowess and creativity in wealth creation. And certain systemic dogmas and self indictments that limit individual liberty to access wealth generation media, even though eerie.

Every man possesses his individual creative abilities, and every sustainable wealth comes from creative ideas mastered. Now your ability to focus, master and channel your creative ideas sets you apart in the scheme of things. It is only wise to realize that the only vital tool for putting all these together and bringing them to bear is *"questions!"*

But I must admit, most of the answers you are looking for are intensively addressed in chapter 6 of this book, QUESTIONS YOU ARE NOT ASKING. In this chapter however, I want to help you understand why the questions that lead to the answers in that chapter are important.

### The Power of Questioning...

> "The power to question is the basis of all human progress"
> Indira Gandhi

You don't have the right to answers whose questions you've not asked. You use questions to challenge your money beliefs. Then you take a bearing of where you were to where you are presently, hence you chart the course for your future with money. Like I said, the most apt tool for navigating these arenas can only be provocative questions. Don't miss that!

Questions are the seed for answers. The more we ask and meditate upon, the much further we get moving in the direction of the realization of our goals... money, or whatever else they may be.

Questions, especially meditative ones and those which quickly spur us into thinking\action help to quickly eliminate distractive and irrelevant options that may be clogging in the way of reaching our goals. And I've dedicated the last and second to the last chapters of this book to address and really share some of the questions and methods you should be applying.

It not only brings clarity and focus, it helps set us in the part of success already. Because, I've leant; for you to start moving in the direction of success, you must first get on the path. And then before even the arrival can be anticipated!

Most of the ways of life are very difficult to understand, and we are left wondering "how"? And in answering the "how" question, we are led to stumble into diverse reasons to explain it away.

So that occasionally we arrive at many different answers, and although most of them may not be very apt at answering the posed question, they give us a wider range of possible outcomes. Some of which may even be right for other scenarios. You see the crucial importance of questioning!

That is why we consider questions very important, more important than answers, primarily because of the foregoing rationale.

Answers are basically always restrictive to specific areas, but more possibilities lies with questions.

Georg Cantor agrees, as he says: *"… the art of proposing a question must be held of higher value than solving it."*

Another Eugene Ionesco comments thus… *"It is not the answer that enlightens, but the question."*

We basically learn more from asking than we do with answers.

Utilizing the tools of self meditation, quarantine and analysis can be major money making wisdom. That is of course if you are talking in respect to wealth creation.

Over the years certain spot-on and apt maxims has been a great source of insight and inspiration in helping me take a hold of some deep facts about myself and life. And they usually do for all of us... at least I'm sure of those who will pay attention.

Often what we really need are insights that will take us on an adventure into the life we've never envisioned or experienced, and facts we didn't know were there, but somehow they just impress on us the idea that we can become more, and that it's actually possible to! Adventure, not into the mountains, space or poles.... But into the possibilities, ideas and creativities lurking within us unexplored.

And there too, lies the possibility for wealth creation, money generation. I believe that.

Never ask questions that put you on hold. Cherish those that spur you into action. I really don't want you to misconstrue my recommendation of 'questioning' for a reason for inaction. Often the best way to approach this is to mutter to oneself these questions, taking cognizance of your inner impressions, because with that, it won't be difficult to figure out the right bid.

Never lazy around and relapse because you want to rationalize. Rationalization is not my emphasis here. Because often, the best moves you'll ever make are those for which you didn't think about. *Something like, the best answers you get are often those for which you didn't put any questions for. Yea, sometimes you just act without asking.*

Prior to this though, a mastery has got to have been created, often subconsciously. You just know, and because you just know, you trust in the outcome. Guts! Have you ever sensed that some things just run as routine in your life that you almost always know the moves to make? I think sometimes we dwell so much on the camouflage of planning, praying, and meditating that we miss out on our best moments.

**Make the moves, examine later. But, examine you must!**

## Create something that's you.

The concept of creative energy as it relates to wealth accumulation is a force that can mainly be appreciated and subsequently activated from the vintage of brokenness. Because it's not all those who's got it going for them that will appreciate its role (the role of brokeness, pain and suffering), and essence in generating substance.

As a matter of fact, most of those who have got it going for them never see that as an asset. At least that hasn't been their experience. And the strategy those people, or writers of such books proffer are equally true depending on which experiences you've had with life.

But for individuals who've been on the down side of life, broken and despised for what they don't yet have going for them…. But who at the same time senses that they've got some unique gifting and ability lurking within them, who know they can become much more, and who as a matter of fact feel that if anybody should be rich it might as well be them. Then this material is designed for them.

It is one thing to have the head knowledge that you are special, and a different ball game altogether to begin to produce results that compensates for your high hopes. (That is why I wrote *EXPRESSIVE POTENTIAL*. You should get the book @ *bennethfelix.com,* it's a good read.)

My point actually is that your money is in your specialty and abilities.... And your ability to focus and effectively channel those, gains you your rewards; in money. This book is not so much focused on creativity and boosting potentials. To learn about how to activate your creative instincts, and gain profit from your potentials, you need to read my other two books. *UNLOCKING YOUR PERSONAL CREATIVITY; MASTERING THE SCIENCE OF SELF ACTUALIZATION and EXPRESSIVE POTENTIAL.* (As I mentioned above).

Those are the most important books you will ever read as far as personal development is concerned. To place an order, contact us here: 2348163724106 or bennefelix.bf@gmail.com and get your personal copies!

The bid to create something that's you is a bid to explore your true self, your innate abilities and potential as a tool for wealth creation. Not every money coach generally sees the wisdom in this recommendation. But I guess every one of us only appreciates life and the lessons, based on the experiences we've had with life. You are right for your experiences with life. And often, you find that your ideals revolve around such experiences. That is a general truth that you must appreciate.

You can trace the wealth of any man you know to something they love, and something they are good at. They you tell you the same!

*What I'm just saying is that we should all learn to use our unique experiences with life to further the course of our life. That requires recognizing opportunities, circumstances that address issues that are related to our story and special needs...* therefore *making the channeling of energy easier.*

So we know that it is more important to pursue vision than to pursue methods and dogmas. And vision in this context is where you see yourself excelling at the most, and or, where you know you can excel at most.

We never get to understand ourselves completely. And quit coming up with the idea that you know "you." That this is completely what you are about and nothing more-.

Although, sound logic admonishes that; and we do. Only, there is still more to us than we are acquainted with. And we must accept that, and give ourselves that room to be worth more.....

What such ideal does is give you room to explore, and to become more without doubts or hesitation.

*The motivation for reaching is in the possibilities of the unknown.*

Give yourself room to believe for more, to be more, to reach for more and expect more.

And be reminded in the words of Sam Adeyemi that:

"Those who are driven by vision will always be more successful than those driven by survival."

# CHAPTER 2

STRATEGIZING  FOR  MORE  MONEY

People who grow in wealth I've learnt are individuals who are always thinking in terms of the next level. By constantly looking unto the next level, looking out for opportunities for growth, you avoid waste, and lassitude. Making the best use of the opportunity and resources you have at hand. This is important.

And there are a couple of tools I think that will be essential in harnessing your wealth generation goals. Please note they are valuable tools as far as this subject is concerned, but they are not finite!

So, we shall be considering…. **TIME, MIND, & DESIRES OR PASSION.**

And because we are using questions as a facilitator in this subject we shall be analyzing shortly what role time, mind and passion play in wealth creation. I just want to mention that indeed they are valuable tools of wealth creation; when maximized of course.

## Time resource:

So the question you should be asking after realizing that time is a vital tool for wealth creation is; and this is well addressed in the last chapter!

How do I recalibrate my time usage for better money creation avenues?

How and where do I focus more of my time for better money creation opportunities?

Where do I need to be making consistent deposits of time in line with my money agenda?

Pay attention to the ideas you come up with, and start doing those things. How much you are able to create in your life rises and fall with time.

People should look at what you are doing, how you spend your time and tell where you're going: or whether or not you are going somewhere important. **Sustainable wealth is created over time; it's a wealth that grows.**

In other words, money usually only grows! If that is the case – that means it grows over time and in time. As I've since learnt, it is the velocity of money that creates wealth. How much can you get done in the shortest possible time?

*That means you are separated from your money goals not necessarily by a number of years, by a number of productive relevant ACTIONS.*

Therefore, you can simply conclude that time is a valuable tool in wealth creation. But actions have a way of compressing time to your advantage.

Hence an effective utilization of any available time must be taken into cognizance in your quest for wealth creation. The more time you waste or play around with, the more money you lose. And the longer it takes to create the wealth that you desire.

As it appears, time is an asset and can be invested: A very vital resource in achieving goals. And I mentioned earlier that you must insist on questioning how you spend your time and see whether or not you are making an adequate use of it.

**How and where do I focus more of my time for better money making opportunities?** That is the question.

That's the question that must be ringing continuously in your head. Every minute gone is time invested or wasted depending on whether or not you make it work for you.

And it doesn't take knowledge of calculus or financial expertise to have your time invested judiciously for greater results. It's as simple as always thinking in terms of what are the next few moves that will make a difference in my life and then giving your time to get them done.

That also means making moves that adds up to your future targets. Especially in developing and mastering your special prowess, and exercising your special ability with more of the time at your disposer. That's how you invest your time!

*The amount of money that flows to you is tied to the mastery of your special prowess, and the ability to create a channeling of it in areas the sell.*

**Spend Your Time Intentionally**

If you must be more productive and resourceful, and therefore generate more money in the future – spend most of your time focused on your strengths; working and mastering your special abilities. This all actually becomes possible with time; as in, over time. But the point I'm emphasizing here is; learn to shrink the time for what you're involved in.

The amount of money that comes to you i

Directly related to how much Time you Spen

On your areas of brilliance, areas of interest and prowess

And one Andy Stanley would say, **"Small deposits of time over time in the areas of your interest make all the difference in your life."**
Because of course, money does answer to prowess, talents and special abilities.

Again to answer the question of; how, where do I invest more of my time…" simply put: invest it on working at your special strengths, invest it exercising your special skills. Every skill, ability gets better by use not by chance!

## Mind resource:

"Money is only an idea. If you want more money,

Simply change your thinking.

Every self made person started small with an idea,

and then turned it into something big."

Robert Kiyosaki.

"…all achievement, all earned riches have their beginning in an idea." Napoleon Hill.

The mind indeed is a great resource especially when it comes to bringing things to reality. Your greatest force to articulate and create lies in your mind. If you are able to manage it well, you'll generate tremendous life changing leverage for yourself.

What I'm saying is, if you can't create it in your mind you can't have it in your life, whatever it is you desire. Usually you should **start out first**

**investing in your mind before you can ever start investing with it.** Hence, treat her with reverence, understanding what great resource it is in moving you to the next level of your life. **Articulate!**

Every one of us have been given the gifts of 'mind and time', as tools for furthering the course of our life. It is up to you to do what you please with both. It'syour choice!

With each money bill that enters your hand, you and only you have the power to determine your destiny. Spend it foolishly and you choose to be poor. Spend it on liabilities and you join the middle class. Invest it on your mind and learn how to acquire assets, and you will be choosing wealth and a secured future.

The choice is yours and only yours. Every day with every penny, you decide to be rich or not. You are the creator of your own destiny. Don't you just like the sound of that?

There is a level of transformation that comes with expanding the capacity of the mind, and understanding that every tangible creation or acquisition was first conceived, molded in the mind before (with consistent mind exercise) it materializes physically. As it was mentioned in The Secret, "wealth is a mindset."

And Napoleon Hill summarized it thus; **"whatever the MIND of man can conceive and believe it can achieve."**

## Desires and Passion:

"Those who are driven by vision will always be more successful than those driven by survival."
Sam Adeyemi

What is it that drives you, to articulate, to create impart and to believe you can? Is it your gifts and abilities? Well, I want to put it to you that it's not so much what you can do as it is the passion you have wrapped around it. That driving force that keeps you restless, pushing you to display…. What you focus on expands. And what you consistently focus on with passion is what you create and become.

With that said, you must decide what you want to create in your life, what special abilities you've got to match that, and then pay close attention to mastering them and on how to channel them effectively. As a matter of fact that is where the challenge lay, the channeling.

Most people can't manage channeling their desires into avenues of greater essence, and for the appropriate course. More so, what does your passion go for, and how strong is it compared to other things?

As much as possible: pay adequate attention to where your greatest desires lie and keep it thus.Follow your bliss, is a life long advice and it still holds true today especially for folks who desire to resolve the puzzles in their life.

A gripping desire and passion takes away the stress of work, making the journey smooth sailing. The route to wealth creation is already tedious as it is; I wouldn't mind taking the smoothest route so long it's safe, assured and ethical. That is shrinking time for you. **But we also need to learn how to shrink stress and the pain of achievement.**

What we've failed to realize over the years is that life is a journey and that the journey is the destination. So where you are is where you're going. The process is the destination. You'll redefine you're life when you are driven to travel in the path you choose.

Find what you love and follow through!

# CHAPTER 3

# CREATING MONEY DISCIPLINE

## Saving and investment purses

Habits have a way of shaping our experiences; as a matter of fact they basically influence and determine how our lives result. Conversely, you are where you are now because of your habits. And your financial state at the moment is a result of your habits with money. The key is; if you are not impressed with the results you are seeing in your life now, you simply change your habits. It takes discipline but it's possible. With time every goal can be achieved!

And what is a habit?

An action done regularly, repeatedly and automatically, often without a conscious thinking. It is your consistent pattern of lifestyle.

Have you ever considered that maybe your lifestyle is hampering your ability to create riches? Maybe that is what's at stake now in reshaping your experiences with money!

In this session, I want to talk to you about cultivating some money habits that will change the direction of you financial life. And if you can insist on mastering them you'll be developing some new life changing habits altogether.

## Cultivating a saving and investment habit

The majority of people I know are all interested in getting wealthy, but very few in this list are actually planning on it, and fewer persons still

are actually going to make it rich. Why? Because it is not only the desi
to be rich that gets you rich or, that you need, almost everybody I kno
desires to be rich. Desire in generating money is only the awakening
moment. But only staying awake won't do, you have to develop the
lifestyle.

And there are certain basic concepts that can kick-start your journey
towards creating wealth. But in this context I'll be addressing "savings
and investing", the most essential tools of the world richest
personalities.

That's where it all starts right? Yes of course! Although, like I earlier
mentioned; the primary pattern people associate with money is
spending. They work, spend, go broke, and work harder some more;
and so the cycle continues.

Generally, most people refuse to realize that becoming rich is always
intentional. You don't stumble into it, (and I used to think I could
stumble into money!) although you can't always determine how, but
you must learn to appreciate the fact that work is required, not
indolence.

This goes to say however that wealth and riches follow a pattern. And
the habits, mindset and beliefs you have about money play a key part.
Alongside cultivating a savings and investment habit, and employing
yourself, your talents and gifts where necessary.

Your life and financial state today is a result of your past habits, (at
least that's what they teach us), and especially belief with money. So i
you want to change your results, you should change your habit,
especially in the area you are trying to improve.

For instance, instead of saying it is difficult to get money, you hold the
belief that it's very easy to prosper. Instead of saying there's not

enough money to go around, you say there is abundance everywhere and that yours is coming to you.

It will not automatically appear so, things might even become intense, but it's a start!

Like I've come to learn, wealth is always intentional, you don't stumble into it. And I have said that saving and investing what we have is a basic step towards creating wealth. So that you must cultivate the habit of saving if you are out on this quest! I'll show you how in the preceding lines....

Before that though, may I mention that you can only determine where you are going by what you are doing now, your daily routine! Now for the trait;

In the end it all boils down to this simply, and I'll let T. Harv Eker, a millionaire and financial guru, explicate that, he says;

> "If you want to get rich, focus on making, keeping, and investing your money. If you want to be poor, focus on spending your money."

And there's no truer truth to that. Most of the times in life, *its not that we don't know what to do, it's our inability to get done what we know should be done.* And I learnt my lessons.

And if you never get to so much read anymore books on money, but goes ahead to practice that quote, you'll increase your financial status exponentially.

### The Savings Habit:

You can use the following ideas to start yourself into the savings habit..

1. ***Change your beliefs about money;*** belief is the guide that takes you to the place of your target. It is your resolute acceptance of something as fact or true, and therefore basing your actions around such beliefs. Your judgments, awareness and level of progression in life are all tied to your believe system. So that your experiences in life are essentially limited to what you believe are ideal or obtainable or not. And that also affects your relationship with money.

   I've already mentioned some of the faulty believes people have about money. And it is these believe patterns that breed such poor handling and experiences in life. You've probably heard the saying, "change your thinking change your life."That is also applicable to beliefs, and it's true in any facet of life! ***To change how you live, you've got to change how you believe.***

   When it comes to this subject, our parents are rarely the best models. They were at most probably poor at handling money, and generally didn't create any healthy perspective for us towards money, so we grow up with a poor default approach towards money.
   I'll recommend you read T. Harv Eker's book, *Secrets of the Millionaire Mind*, there you'll learn how to reprogram your money beliefs.

   Remember I mentioned that for the majority of people, especially in the African culture, we assume that the primary purpose of money is to be spent. So when they get any, they spend it!

However, you can do more with your money than spend it, especially if your target is to come out of poverty. And there is time for spending. But you can't be living above your means and expect to amass wealth. So you must decide on your own to change that believe pattern.

2. **Think through:** "the fact is that your character, your *THINKING* and your beliefs are critical part of what determines your success." Says Mr. Harv.
Your thoughts are very crucial elements in the formation of your beliefs and life realities.
That is why it's a basic in the creation of healthy money habits and for your wealth generation. Learn how to associate only empowering thoughts when it comes to money, its important! And actually think before you spend.

So to help in your new habit of saving, the next time money comes to your hand don't rush into spending it, 'think:' "what other purposes can I use this money for? How can I make it grow?" When you think of other means of expending your money instead of just spending them away, you create value for your money, a value which shall be compensated for adequately.

3. **Cut your frivolous expenses:** success of any kind requires some personal sacrifices and self denial. You can't have it your way all the times and build anything substantial.

## Create a financial plan:

"If you want to be rich, you must know what

Kind of income to work for, how to keep it

And how to protect it from lose."

Robert Kiyosaki

Your money must have a goal and a direction, and it is your onus to make it so. When you create a focus for the usage of your earnings it becomes more resourceful and multiplying.

Make room for the money you want in your life, and strategize on how to keep it when it comes. I know you want more money; we get up every day needing more. But for most people, especially broke folks that's all there is to it. They only know they need more and never consider keeping it or making the much they have at hand grow. Intend it....

You must intend on building the knowledge of, and understanding the functionalities of money: what they call financial intelligence. Don't just set your mind on the ability to generate money, go all the way through, and think about keeping your money. And you can't do that if you don't plan for it.

This is a knowledge I first came in terms with in my mid twenties with no much bills in my name. But having that consciousness and building on it is making a tremendous difference in my financial life.  Because we always only have the tendency to spend and usurp every little penny that comes in handy we fail to explore other valuable means of sustainable application.

So what are some of the basic financial plans you can apply to your life?

**THE MONEY QUESTION.**
                                                     **???**

**First, understand how money works: become financially astute!** The world of money is a system of its own, an institute worthy of learning of. And because money comes with a spirit, or that it has a spirit to it,

you need to learn to master that spirit!

**Map out a Savings and *Investment* pocket for your every earning:** With emphasis to investing. The money you invest multiplies that which you save only accumulates.

**Money discipline:** it takes discipline to make things work. Not so much motivation or inspiration. What happens when the going gets tough, most of the times it takes discipline to push through.

**Seasonal money targets:** always check out your pace of progression financially. What they call budgeting! Have a budget and work by it.

# CHAPTER 4

## Money Only Grows

As obvious as this may seem, money is not always treated in that light. We assume it is "gotten" basically. Gotten as in; we have the head knowledge that we are going to be rich, so we make no plans for it: at most we'll decide to save.

**But whatever grows is also cultivated, tended to, nurtured and sown with an end expectation of growth. That is to say it is an intentional act. So that if you don't commit to growing your money you either lose it or waste it.**

Often and generally, people think that the purpose of money is to be spent, so they do! And then wear themselves out wondering why they are broke and poor. "How can I be making or having this level of money coming to me all the time and yet remain broke at the same time?"

To them, even as I used to think; someone will just knock at their door some day and present them some papers saying: "you are the next millionaire." Trust me; you'll wait forever!

Actually, the ability to make money is a mind thing. You really need to change your thinking and believes about money in order to begin to experience a different result: because those influence your outcome. And I've been quite outspoken about this throughout this book!

So the next time money comes to your hand instead of spending; think. Ask yourself what other possible uses you could put the cash at hand into that will ensure it grows and generates some more money, not immediately but over time.

I've already mentioned that money grows with time…. It doesn't just happen. By the way; the primary purpose of money is not to be spent; (again!) only the poor think and do so.

## Seeds of investment

No doubt you are probably aware of the popular caution usually from preachers. They say; "if the money you have at hand is not enough for what you want to use it for, sow it." You know about the concept right, maybe not! However, it seems striking and may easily arouse your acceptance.

Well, the principle is true. As a matter of fact it is a biblical concept. Sowing that is! Consider 2Corinthians 9:10.

*He that gives seed to the sower also gives food, and multiplies the seed you sow and increases your harvests* .Author's version

Usually, seeds are smaller version of the harvest. Anything that has the potential to multiply its kind can be described as a seed. And for people planning on wealth creation, you'll agree that the money you have at hand now is not all the money you need.

And it can hardly afford most of the things you need, so in that form you know that what you have is a seed. And if you are expectant of more, and only have a seed, what do you do? You sow it! That's what seeds are for; sowing, investing, and planting.

So I agree that if the money you have at hand is a seed (can't afford what you need ;) sow it. Only I don't think sowing means (or only means) giving it away. And I'm a giver! I am for giving. And giving is one of the spiritual laws of money as I will explain at a later chapter.

But when you insist on always giving your seeds away, you leave your wealth life to chance. And I've said you don't become wealthy by chance or by some supernatural intangible force alone, but you can too – receive supernatural supplies. But we must come to appreciate the fact that life is practical and requires a practical approach.

Now you must learn to invest your money (which is an act of sowing) into grounds that are realistic and has operational media of returns. **By taking cognizance of where your money is entering and for what purpose, you determine your future with money.**

So let every decision you make with regards to any money that comes in handy be an informed, predetermined decision. One geared towards expanding your wealth creation opportunities.

*Don't think 'spending' every time you get some money, that's not the primary purpose of money. Don't think giving it away, that's not all there is to seed sowing. Think investing, think incremental saving, and think making your money grow!*

By that singular act, you set yourself apart for wealth creation!

# CHAPTER 5

# THE CURSE OF EASE

*"The more you protect yourself from losing money, the more you protect yourself from making money."*

Robert kiyosaki

Have you realized how much people crave an easy and comfortable life? Well everyone desires some comfort, and that's ok. At the same time, the craving for comfort is one of the major setbacks keeping people from actually growing rich. **You can't tiptoe your way to any significant success!**

This is because to actually grow rich, you need to expand your capacity to create wealth. That requires a high level of sacrifice and self denial. That requires giving up stuff, most of which you have attached so much sentiment and pride in.

Conversely, expanding your capacity for wealth creation means treading the tough routes, reaching for unfamiliar zones and sometimes making unusual moves! Simply put; the high life is not an easy life!

Your comfort zone never allows you grow to a stretch. As the quote below suggests:

"To grow as a person you have to expand your comfort zone. The only time you can actually grow rich is when you are outside your comfort zone." T. Harv Eker

If you are too careful, you end up a victim of circumstances. A little pain is necessary for realizing your money dreams. But if you insist on playing it so safe that you never miss a mark, you just never know! But what I think is, you end up turning your precautions into a curse that hampers your productivity instead.

If you asked me, I'd say, stop getting obsessed with taking things easily all the time. You need grit. And you need to go after the money you want in your life fearlessly, but passionately!

**MONEY IS A MEASURE OF VALUE**

To be living in ease is to be lacking in value. Because when you are sure of your self, you shed all biases, you gain boldness and confidence to do, and those are important keys in laying your financial concerns to rest.

So that you then realize that money flows to you in commensuration to your values. The more valuable you become, the more money answers to you, and you have to risk putting those values out to be recognized and gain the rewards they deserve.

More money flows to the person who offers the most value. Take the market place for instance, usually you don't receive more pay, because of age or longevity, but for what solutions you proffer, & problems you solve.

People grow in the corporate ladder by value not by grace. Even when grace answers to you, you still need capacity to sustain what you have been freely given. But it's a tough climb up the corporate ladder; you must needs lose certain comforts to go that up.

A colleague of mine shared a thought in this regard that I'd like pass to you:

"Money is not wealth. Printing more of it does not make the society richer. Money is an instrument of value, like a scale or a clock.

Meaning; the amount of money present indicates the amount of value present at the location - genuine money I mean.

However, getting more money is simply synonymous to housing more value and pitching them to the right audience.

Wealthy and monetary richness go head to tail; you can't be wealthy with value and lack the equivalent money to flaunt. Money is like volcanic eruption leading to the consistently solidified igneous source beneath. Like volcanic eruption money flows in after a lot of never-ending work on the background and then the obvious eruption serving as a pointer to the work.

The Productive make money a measuring instrument of their progress. Don't be deceived, you'll be rich or productive the moment you're wealthy with enough value (I mean problems solving value). "

Zion Bassey

Once you understand the difference, you liberate yourself from the plaguing curses of ease and over cautiousness.

# CHAPTER 6

## QUESTIONS YOU ARE NOT ASKING

**WHAT ARE THE PHYSICAL LAWS OF MONEY?**

Life is practical. A mystical approach will leave you with nothing, as you will make every effort to leave everything to chance. And I often thought it was a sin to apply a practical sense to life. It always had to be "faith." So I constantly contradicted myself, because on the other hand I also believed there was such a thing as cause and effect.

My mindset completely changed about this when I heard one of my heroes say, "...life is practical not mystical. Therefore, we have to give a practical approach in other to make the most of our adventure on earth."He said, "I believe a mystical approach will produce a miserable end." That was Bishop David Oyedepo. And this is one of the "godliest" and spiritual men I know.

These are your, or should I say, *'OUR'* practical clues for financial affluence. It is following through that makes all the difference, when you resolve to learn and follow through, the principle answers to you.

**Savings:** saving is a physical law of money that connotes the following;

To store for future use, to economize, to conserve and prevent excessive use or wastage, and to cause to accumulate. There are certain future needs that are worth preparing for; saving for such cannot be displaced. We all have future plans and expectations, and most of those future goals are generally things money will cater for. As a matter of fact, often it is really for the scarcity of money that we have future goals, so when you save you are saying, "I believe in the future, my future is possible."

**Investment:** this means the setting aside of a sum, to enable the accumulation of more. To commit money into something, or to spend money for the purpose of increase or profit, or some benefit. I am going to explain more on expectation soon. Investment yields returns in multiples not in additions.

The mistake the majority of people make in failing to adopt the strategy of investment include:

*The belief that investment is for some acclaimed sect*

*There's not enough capital*

*It's not real*

*You can lose your money. Etc!*

**Value transference:** money increases with value. As a matter of fact, money is a means of exchange of values. So if you want money you must have some value to offer. The more value you possess, and the valuable you become, the more your command and in command of money you become.

**Work:** and the master says; he that will not work let him not eat. Work is the most basic medium for monetary reward. A worker is worthy of his wages, even the universe respects and honor that. When you work, you set yourself in an automatic queue for financial rewards. The 9/5 formula is no joke. That is how our entire systems are organized, and it is working, working because everybody respects it and believes in it.

Get involved in a work, get a job, start from there and then grow up.

**Services:** this has to do primarily with the buying and selling of products until they are consumed, after production of course. And this is one vital way of generating money, because after production, or buying, you sell for a profit. And the profit is to your advantage.

But you have to read this, someone once taught me that *if you are ever going to be rich, you have to sell something, buy something or do something.* And that made a huge difference in my life. Guess who taught me that... No way? I will tell you, it was Kim. That's right, Kim Kiyosaki !

**Selling and Buying:** that's just what i said, buy, sell, do something and trigger the flow of money.

### WHAT ARE THE SPIRITUAL LAWS OF MONEY?

Even in the spiritual realms, there are forces at play, forces which can either work for or against you, depending on how you decide to wield them. I call these spiritual because you really can not explain how they work, or why they work, or their manner of operations. But this one thing is certain, they work.

**Giving:** giving is an eternal spiritual law of divine supplies, it has always been! If you are lacking in giving, you will be lacking in receiving. It's that simple.

It is first seed time, before harvest. If you aren't therefore sowing seeds in terms of "Giving", how then do you plan on receiving?"...for whatsoever a man sows that shall he also reap."Galatians 6:7.

Genesis 8:22 "While the earth remains, seedtime and harvest, and cold and heat, and summer and winter, and day and night shall not cease."

So you see, it's not just me saying it, it is a divine spiritual law for getting or better still, receiving anything you want.

**Anticipation:** expect what you are asking for. Expect your desires to come through, if you leave everything vague or to chance, you won't be sure of what's turning up. And you very likely might not get anything in return. Take that from me. Besides, that's what your imagination is for.

Always expect prosperity to come while and after you have invested the other seeds. Expect the amount of money you want, and how often you need it to keep flowing. If you make it clear and vivid enough, it will show up for you.

**Spoken word:** everything hears. There's power in spoken words, you speak in terms of declarations for summoning what you want. If you want it, you say it. Whether or not you have paid your dues, and therefore feel entitled to what's coming, still say it out. And especially when you have paid your dues, declare what you want, declare what you deserve, and declare what's coming to you. The plan of the enemy is to shut you up, by giving you a sense of entitlement.

Speak what you want to see, have or do. There's power in what you say.

Call forth what you want to see... Calling those things that "be" not as though they were. It is written in the book of wisdom that, "a man shall be satisfied with good by the fruit of his mouth...."

## WHAT ARE THE PSYCHOLOGICAL LAWS OF MONEY?

**Mind:** your mind is the most important tool when it comes to the creation or manifestation of anything, including and especially money.

Everything is first accomplished in the mind before it is accomplished physically. If you can't use your mind constructively, you lose a considerable percentage of your life. Anything your mind can't handle, your hands can't handle. Which means any sum you can't see yourself possessing mentally, you will NEVER have in your life.

Your life expands or stagnates in direct measure to your mental capacity.

What you don't use you lose. The highest good you can do for yourself is to develop your mind, by that I mean, developing your mental capacity. Imagine big things, see big things, expect big things, and get your mind consistently exposed to big things. Once you do this consistently, after a while, big things begin to show up in your life.

**Imagination:** imagination means your mental pictures. The mind is a mental tool; imagination is your mental activities. That is how you use the mind. Imagination is the use of the mind to picture the things you want in your life, how you want your life to turn out, the sum of money you want, when you want it etc. It's important you do this, and form the routine. That is what changes your life.

**Visualization**: the mind, imagination and visualization go together. Visualization means to mentally SEE your self in possession of, and using the things or money you'll like to have in your life. With emphasis on *SEEING*! Picture the whole process for yourself, and see them all **playing** out.

**Beliefs and Mental disposition**: some people's set beliefs and disposition about money is just plane wrong, and faulty, so much that they will never amass money, not until those believe patterns are modified and changed.

Take for example, you can't carry around a believe that, being wealthy is bad, evil and unnecessary, or that money is only meant for some few sect and group of persons, or that you can never be wealthy, or that you are destined to be poor etc. You can't carry around this set of belief patterns and still expect to attract money.

You can't attract what you don't admire and intensely crave, not even money. Money is like a pretty maiden; she must be wooed and attracted. Your beliefs determine how you lead, and what you attract to your life. When you change your beliefs (especially those negative and dysfunctional ones), you change your life.

**Thoughts:** what are you thinking about? Are they empowering or demeaning thoughts? Someone has said you should think about what you're thinking about. That means, watch your thoughts, especially those that negate the money consciousness you are trying to build. Again, your thoughts are the actual images your mind focuses on per time. It is your seat of contemplation and formation.

In general, what I'm trying to get you to come to the consciousness of is that your mental processes play a huge part in your financial life, what you get, how much and how often you get it and how what you get serves you.

By mental-processes I mean your Mind which is the seat of your mental processes. Then your imaginations, visualization, beliefs and mental disposition - by mental disposition I mean the state of your mind per time, or your preconditioned state of thinking, how you usually think, the kind of thoughts that hover within your mind most. And then your thoughts, which are the actual images you hold in your mind.

## WHAT ARE THE INTANGIBLE LAWS OF MONEY ?

This is a money source which can put some money into your pocket, yet it is not an automatic avenue for getting money, hence "intangible."They include:

**GIFTS AND FAVOR**

**BORROWING**

**And INHERITANCE**

But note, like I said earlier; while all these can be media for generating or raising money, they are not really substantial financial avenues, because they rely so much on the other person's judgments, likeness, capability, etc. What I mean is they are not really based on actual predictable steps, so that it is a tricky resolve to rely so much on the intangible sources of financial success.

And people do gain money like this, and often make the most of it, in other cases it doesn't turn out so well. The consequences for mishandled borrowing for instance can be fatal, and the success can be mouth watering too, just tread with caution. Focus on money laws you can influence!

## HOW DO I BOOST MY EARNING ABILITY?

The financial ladder according to Jim Rohn has already been build or established; the only way to move up and earn more is to increase in value.

So there is need no doubt to always find ways to climb this ladder, you do that basically by getting better, and seeking for ways to get better and become better at what you do. You do that by boosting you market values. And you do that by taking hold of the following....

**LEARN A SKILL,** it's either you are growing or you are stuck. "More" is better than "single." Get better. Skills say you are worth more....And if you have the time and means, its ok or say, better to learn more than one skill. That's the key!

**DEVELOP YOUR GIFTS AND TALENT,** you'll be surprised to know that your gifts and talents were giving to you for profiting, not for leisure, show off or to impress others. (That surprises you right? Lol!)

Anyways, you can make the most of whatever innate abilities you've been given, but you must develop them, raise them to the highest standard of relevance, and they will serve you in ways you never imagined.

There are so many people who play around with their talents, so many, and they fail to see the money in it. If you are going to learn anything from these pages today, learn this; *there's money in your prowesses.* Stop playing around.

In my book **EXPRESSIVE POTENTIAL**, I addressed how you can actually overcome being stuck with all the abilities you might have and how to draw gain from them by sharing them with the world in ways that bring about profiting. You can get your personal copy of this book now when you contact me via; **2348163724106, or bennefelix.bf@gmail.com**

**START A BUSINESS,** getting a business running by yourself does a couple of things for you, it enables you control your work space, your pay, time, and of course boosts and keeps you in charge of the amount of money coming to you.

**DO BUSINESS WITH YOUR BUSINESS:** that means, show some discipline in running your business, don't eat or spend everything. Balance your profits effectively, and reinvest, reinvest, reinvest! Don't squash your profits and then expect a miracle to happen to cover up. We must learn to live life in a practical approach.

**INCREASE IN VALUE,** as simple as that sounds, do it. In the end, that's where it all boils down to. The more valuable you become, the more money flows to you. You can do this by adopting some of the few strategies I suggested earlier, learn a skill, develop your innate abilities, get more education, accept responsibilities, solve more problems etc.

I have only stated it out here so that you can make it intentional. Be intentional about building values and increasing in values, don't wish, pray or mystify anything about it. Just go out and get better.

**PROFER SOLUTION TO PROBLEMS;** Become a problem solver. That is also one way of increasing in value. *Don't run or hide yourself in difficult times, don't make excuses, find the answer, and find the way.* When you become the one who always find a way and always resolve complications, people look at you differently.... That also means better financial treatments.

**MARKETING:** market everything of value you have, anything you have to offer that meet people's needs is worth marketing. There's someone who needs what you have, share it with them, let the word out. Nobody will patronize you if they don't know your service exists.

The more people know about you, the more patronage, hence; the more money.

## WHY ARE SOME PEOPLE MORE SUCCESSFUL THAN OTHERS ?

This is a question that can be easily answered on the basis of the psychological laws of money, as explicated above. Everything is first created mentally before it materializes physically.

So it is our mental processes that make the most difference in the financial states of people. And of course, the effects of the law of cause and effect play out too. Are you being diligent to the basic physical laws of money? Investment, saving, or work for instance. Poverty or riches are all states of mind, if your state of mind predominantly read riches, you attract wealth, because you do things that create wealth, and this may even start out unconsciously. If poor, you attract the same effect of poverty, lack and want. Because you also adopt lifestyles that keep money from you, as simple as that!

## WHY DOES THE RICH KEEP GETTING RICHER?

The rich keep getting richer because they have gained a mastery of their mental states, which has already been conditioned for wealth and success. The truth is, if you think you can, you can. But let it be clear here that they don't just wish and think, they also have a strong work ethics - they work creatively and in line with their areas of passion, so they enjoy work and never get tired.

In addition, they are grittier, more focused and desperate in their pursuits. When they go for a thing, they go all in.

The problem with most of us is that we think success is cheap, that we don't have to try so hard, that we 'deserve' to get whatever we ask for whenever we ask for it. So we generally get upset and feel obliged to

get offended with life if we don't see things going our way at our pac
so we give up.

Conversely, the most successful amongst us, persevere and persist
more, so they win more... with their already established empowering
states of mind.

## WHAT IS THE SECRET OF MONEY?

The secret of money is basically tied to solving problems, meeting
needs and generally seeking out opportunities to proffer solutions an
help people. When you solve a problem, you create favor, and favor
means more money.

Hold it, not so fast; in line with this secret is also the principle of seed
time and harvest, you have to be a giver. **Don't horde what you get,
share it. When you do, it spreads and returns to you.**

*And then, believe these processes. Back everything you do with faith
and that faith will serve you.*

# CHAPTER 7

## CONFESSIONS AND MEDITATIVE THOUGHTS: MY MONEY MAKING WISDOM.

This is the part where you do it yourself. This is the part where you exercise some of the spiritual laws I taught you earlier. Forget about whether you understand it or believe the process or not. But if you are serious about building a better relationship with money you have to take the following lines seriously.

Meditate when and where you need to, and then speak, imagine and act when you have to and watch the changes begin to take place.

These are the confessions of faith, and meditations you need to adopt to start yourself towards money consciousness and attraction.

- First, I admit I want to increase in wealth! I need to increase my income and money making ability; what do I do? (Clue; self. Focus on self. Increase in value, and provide value. Be more than one thing).

- I realize that I have a wealth generative mind and creative energy….

- **How do I recalibrate my time for better money generating activities?**(consider how you spend your time, where you spend your time most and for what purpose)

- **In light of my past experiences, current circumstances, and future hopes and dreams, where do I need to be making consistent deposits of time?** (Clue; be future minded. Consider how you want to be seen in the nearest future, which areas you want to be featured in and then give more attention into creating that future)

- **What are my money goals?** (Clue; consider, how much you want to make, at what intervals or time frame! How are you going to generate this money, how much will you put aside or invest? How often? What are you going to do or offer in exchange?)

- **What's my strategy for wealth creation?** (Clue; learn a new skill, invest more, save more, explore other profitable fields you might need to go into).

- **How, where do I invest more of my time for better money making opportunities?**(you know yourself, and you should understand the selling points around your vicinity, consider those and determine where you stand a better chance financially).

- **What do I really want?** (Be definite, be clear and be precise about what you really want in, and out of life).

- **What do I want to see done in the next six months?** (In relation to where you want to be financially, plan it out and decide it.)

- **What new outrageous moves can I make this season?** (Every once in a while, try something new, make some unconventional moves!)

- **But what is really money?** (What does money mean to you? A mere paper, a measure of significance, a reward for difference etc. But whatever you come up with, make sure it triggers your passion and waters your drive to generate more, and ensure it is for a worthy purpose)

- **How do I get more money?** (What is your earning ability? Identify the one critical skill that can help generate more money in your present firm)

- **How, where do I invest to generate more money?** (You really need to consider investment as a major source of wealth creation, explore the most profitable investment opportunities around you and take advantage of them as quickly as possible)

- **How does the rich get richer?** (Consider their mindset. Consider their thought processes and model them. The rich and Successful are a unique set of people that the only way to understand them is to study them. Study them!)

Thank you for investing your time in this book. I wish you all the good your desire!

# APPRECIATING YOU

I appreciate you friend. I appreciate you sir. I appreciate you ma. I appreciate you all. Deciding to go through this material is one of the bravest and unbiased moves on the earth today. You've just singled yourself out, proven brave and courageous, my regards!

Precious Benneth my sister, you are a blessing. Thank you to my beautiful and inspiring friend Clara Ebule, your creativity and warmth reception is matchless. And to everyone else who has come through for me throughout this process, you are in my heart. And I thank you!

# Hi, I am Benneth Felix

**I WRITE**

**I SPEAK**

**I ENTERPRISE**

**BOTH BUSINESS AND HUMAN RESOURCES**

**(I HELP INDIVIDUALS EXPLORE THE POSSIBILITIES FOR 'MORE' WITHIN THEM)**

LET'S CONNECT: 08163724106

I would like to hear from you,

how has the book impacted

you or what are your thoughts?

A simple SMS will do!

## Other books by Benneth Felix

1. *EXPRESSIVE POTENTIAL*
2. *UNLOCKING YOUR PERSONAL CREATIVITY: MASTERING THE SCIENCE OF SELF ACTUALIZATION*

3. *DON'T STAY STUCK*
4. *IDENTITY*
5. *PLUNGE*
6. *CORPORATE LEADERSHIP*

*YOU CAN PLACE AN ORDER FOR ANY COPY OF YOUR CHOICE!*

www.ingramcontent.com/pod-product-compliance
Lightning Source LLC
Chambersburg PA
CBHW021512210526
45463CB00002B/993